Managing Editor
Karen J. Goldfluss, M.S. Ed.

Editor-in-Chief
Sharon Coan, M.S. Ed.

Illustrators
Howard Chaney
Bruce Hedges

Cover Artist
Lesley Palmer

Art Coordinator
Kevin Barnes

Art Director
CJae Froshay

Imaging
Ralph Olmedo, Jr.
Rosa C. See

Product Manager
Phil Garcia

Publisher
Mary D. Smith, M.S. Ed.

Weather

SUPER SCIENCE ACTIVITIES

Written by Ruth M. Young, M.S. Ed.

Teacher Created Resources, Inc.
6421 Industry Way
Westminster, CA 92683
www.teachercreated.com

ISBN: 978-0-7439-3667-5

©2002 Teacher Created Resources, Inc.
Reprinted, 2009

Made in the U.S.A.

Table of Contents

Introduction

Life on Earth is possible only because of the envelope of air covering the planet. We call this envelope *atmosphere*, and it is hundreds of miles thick. The atmosphere protects us from the sun's harmful rays and most meteors which may be pulled toward Earth by gravity. The atmosphere is made of gases, mostly *nitrogen* and *oxygen,* but also small amounts of other gases, such as *carbon dioxide*.

Weather affects our lives in many ways—the clothing we wear, the types of homes we need, how we spend our leisure time, and the ways we travel. Weather also often determines our moods—for example, sunshine puts us in a happier mood than overcast skies or rain. It also determines the types of plants and animals that can survive in various areas of the world.

Some parts of Earth receive more heat from the sun than others. The equator receives the greatest amount of sunlight, the poles the least. This uneven heating of Earth's surface causes air movement—that is, the winds. Warm air at the equator moves toward the poles, and cold air at the poles moves toward the equator. Earth's rotation deflects the winds to the west. This regular wind pattern is complicated because Earth's surface is made up of land and water. Land heats up more quickly than water but also loses its heat faster. This sets up pressure differences in the air over various parts of the world. Earth's motion around the sun, causing the seasons, further complicates matters. As a result of all these influences, masses of air wander about Earth's surface. It is these wandering air masses that are responsible for changes in weather. They run into each other and rise as they warm or sink as they cool.

The water on Earth is constantly being recycled through the atmosphere. Water on Earth's surface evaporates into water vapor, a gas, and is held in the air. When the air cannot hold any more moisture, the vapor condenses into water droplets and ice crystals. These form clouds which are carried along by the winds. Depending upon the various conditions of temperature and pressure, rain or snow or other forms of precipitation may fall. Fog is a localized cloud which is sitting on Earth's surface.

The activities in this book enable students to learn about some of the instruments used to measure weather conditions. They will introduce some of the basic concepts of weather patterns, such as the movement of wind and the cloud formations. Most importantly, students will discover that continuous observations are needed to learn about weather conditions where they live.

Watching the Weather

Overview: *Students gather data on daily weather patterns.*

Materials

- large calendar
- weather symbols for the calendar (page 5)
- videotape of TV weather report for the day previous to the closure activity
- transparency and copy of the Student Weather Calendar for each student (page 6)

Activity 1

1. Gather students in the morning and explain that they are going to begin a record of the type of weather they have every day for a month. *Note*: This activity works well if begun at the first of the month and incorporated into the daily calendar routine.

2. Have students tell about different kinds of weather they have experienced. List their ideas on the board. Let volunteers come forward to draw a symbol for each type of weather. Be sure to include terms such as *sunny*, *partly cloudy*, *rainy*, and *snowy*.

3. Show the class the symbols they will use on their weather chart. Compare these to symbols the students drew on the board.

4. Discuss the weather conditions today. If possible, go outside where they can see the sky and help them choose the right symbol to represent the conditions they see. Glue the symbol on today's date on the calendar. Now ask the children to predict tomorrow's weather. Their predictions will be only guesses at this point. On the calendar, pin the symbol which represents the majority predictions for tomorrow's weather.

5. The next morning, have students again report the weather condition and check to see if their predicted symbol was accurate. If not, replace it with the correct one. Repeat this all week until the children feel comfortable using symbols.

Activity 2

1. After students have posted the weather symbols for the week, distribute a Student Weather Calendar to each student. Use the transparency of the chart to help them complete information such as days of the week and dates. Begin their weather calendar with the first of the month.

2. Have students copy data from the class weather calendar onto their own calendars, drawing the weather symbol for each day.

3. Let students draw the weather symbol for the present day on their calendar and post the correct symbol on the classroom calendar. Continue to do this throughout the month. Include the weather for weekends and holidays on both calendars.

4. At the end of each week, discuss the different types of weather students have recorded.

Closure

Show a weather report recorded from the previous day's television broadcast. As it is viewed, point out some information being covered in the report. Ask students to watch the weather report that evening and be ready to tell about it tomorrow.

Watching the Weather *(cont.)*

Weather Symbols

Sunny							
Cloudy							
Partly Cloudy							
Rainy							
Snowy							

Watching the Weather *(cont.)*

Student Weather Calendar

month_____ **year**_____

How Do Thermometers Work?

Teacher Information

Thermometers work on the principal of expansion and contraction of liquids at different temperatures. Thermometers are filled with alcohol dyed red for easy viewing or mercury, which is silver in color. The thermometer is a glass tube sealed at both ends and partially filled with the liquid. Thermometers are calibrated to an exact temperature scale, either in degrees of Fahrenheit (F) or Celsius (C). When it is hot, the liquid inside the thermometer will expand and rise in the tube; the opposite happens when it is cold.

Overview: *Students will learn to read and make their own thermometers.*

Materials

- hot and cold water
- ice
- room-temperature water
- clear plastic nine-ounce (270 mL) cups
- black felt marker
- clear drinking straws
- tacky adhesive (used to adhere pictures to a wall, available in most office supply stores)
- red food coloring
- rubbing alcohol (available in drug stores)
- small clear plastic water bottles with screw-on lids
- nail (the same diameter as the drinking straws)
- hammer
- easy-to-read thermometers (all the same and with both Celsius & Fahrenheit readings)
- transparency which students will use, or the one shown on page 9
- *optional:* trays

Lesson Preparation

- Use the hammer and nail to make a small hole in the center of the lid of the plastic bottle. This hole needs to hold the straw in place without pinching it closed.
- Push the straw through the hole so that it is about $1/2$ inch (1 cm) above the bottom of the bottle. Place tacky adhesive around the straw where it meets the cap so it is airtight.
- Fill the bottle $1/4$ full of alcohol and add a few drops of red coloring.
- Screw the lid on the bottle, making certain it fits tightly. Some of the alcohol may rise in the straw at this point.
- Test the thermometer in hot and ice water. If the hot water makes the alcohol rise so high that it spills out of the straw, pour some out.
- Make sets of three plastic cups. Use a black felt marker to label each set "hot," "cold," and "room temperature." Fill the cups $3/4$ full with water just before the activity. Add ice to the cold water. Be sure the hot water will not burn. These sets may be placed on trays to minimize spilling.

Note: This activity is divided into two parts which may be conducted on different days, if needed.

How Do Thermometers Work? *(cont.)*

Activity 1

1. Ask students what is used to tell the temperature of liquid, air, or their bodies (*thermometers*). Tell them that they are going to use a simulated thermometer to learn how it works.

2. Divide the students into small groups and give each group a set of cups and the bottle thermometer. Explain that the straw is like the glass tube in a real thermometer and that the liquid is alcohol which you dyed red so they could see it.

3. Have the students test their thermometers in the three cups of water and watch what happens to the liquid in the straw each time it is placed into a different temperature.

4. Discuss what they observed. Be sure they see that the liquid rises when it gets hot and drops when it becomes cold.

5. Let students try making the alcohol warm with their own hands to see if their body temperature will register on their thermometers.

6. Tell the students to place their thermometers into the hot water. Ask them what temperature the thermometer is showing. They will realize that they cannot answer the question, since the thermometers show no numbers.

7. Explain that in their next activity, they will learn about real thermometers to compare with those they have just used.

Activity 2

1. Divide the students into small groups and give each group a thermometer. Tell them to examine its parts and be ready to tell you what they see.

2. Discuss what the students saw on their thermometers.

3. Distribute the three sets of water to the students. Have them place their thermometers into the cups, watching to see what happens to the liquid as they do so. Discuss what they observe. Compare this with the bottle thermometers they used in the previous activity.

4. Show the transparency of the thermometers and point out the Celsius (C°) and Fahrenheit (F°) markings. Explain that most countries, other than the United States use a Celsius thermometer because it is part of the metric system. Show the students how to read the thermometer by drawing in a red line and explaining how to read this information for both sides. Point out the markings 0° and 32° and explain that water freezes at 32°F or 0°C and that although these numbers are different, they both represent the freezing point of water. Show the students the body temperature of 98.7° F and compare it to that in Celsius.

5. Let the students return to placing their thermometers into the water cups and reading the temperature from the scale. Have them read both C° and F° temperature of their water. Move among the students to help them with this.

Closure

- Place one of the thermometers on the classroom wall low enough for students to read it. Take two thermometers outside and place one in the sun and the other in the shade. Help students to read these. Discuss why they are all different temperatures.

- Add the outside temperature to the classroom weather calendar, using the thermometer in the shade. Continue to do this daily until the weather calendar is no longer used. Try to record the temperature at the same time each day so it can be compared with the previous day.

How Do Thermometers Work? *(cont.)*

Reading a Thermometer

The temperature on a thermometer is determined by finding the level of the red mercury in the tube and the number on the temperature scale across from it. The temperature is written in numbers with the ° sign. For example, 80° F is read: 80 degrees Fahrenheit.

The **Fahrenheit** scale records the freezing point of pure water at 32° F and the boiling point of water at 212° F (at sea level). The temperature is usually reported in degrees Fahrenheit in newspapers, on the radio, and on television. The normal mouth temperature of the human body is 98.6° F on this scale.

The **Celsius** thermometer records temperatures based on the freezing point of pure water at 0° C and a boiling point of water at 100° C (at sea level). The Celsius thermometer is used in most countries other than the United States because it is part a of a metric system. The Celsius thermometer is usually used by scientists because it is based on a decimal system using multiples of ten. The normal mouth temperature of the human body is 37° C on this scale.

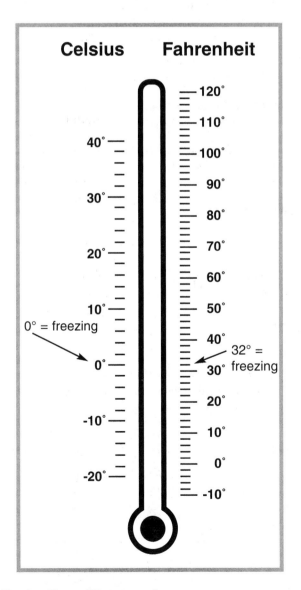
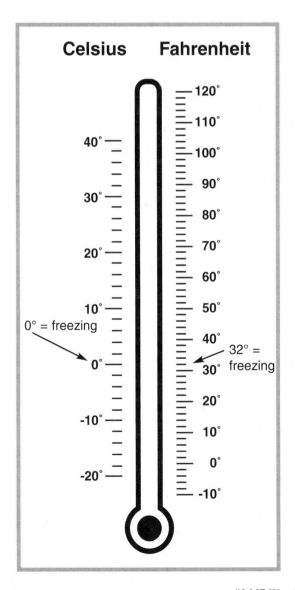

Graphing the Weather

Overview: *Students will graph weather data recorded for one month.*

Materials

- Classroom and Student Weather Calendars from the previous lesson
- videotape of previous evening's TV weather report
- transparency and copies of Weather Graph (page 11)
- copies of Weather Symbols (page 5)
- piece of large white butcher paper, at least 36 inches (90 cm) square
- double-sided tape or glue sticks

Lesson Preparation

- Project the transparency of the weather graph on the butcher paper and trace it to make a large graph. Add additional columns beside the symbols, if needed, for the data to be graphed.
- Make multiple copies of the weather symbols. These will be used to paste on the weather graph, so make enough of each to represent those pasted on the classroom weather calendar. Place these on a table in the classroom.

Activity (This should be done on the last day of the month.)

1. Have students tell about weather reports they saw last evening on TV.
2. Let students post the symbol for today's weather on the classroom and their own weather calendars. Review weather students observed during the month. Tell them they are going to make a graph of the number of days of that month which were sunny, cloudy, partly cloudy, rainy, or snowy in the morning.
3. Divide the students into four or five groups. Assign each group a different week on the weather calendar.
4. Explain that each group should choose the symbols they need for each day of their week from the table where these have been displayed. They should write the corresponding date on each of the symbols. Have the students put double-sided tape or glue on the back of each symbol.
5. After all the weather symbols have been prepared, call one child from each group to post their symbols on the large graph beside the matching symbol shown in the left column.

Closure

- Have students look at the results on the graph and discuss what the weather was like during the month. They should count days for each type of weather pattern and record that on the graph at the end of the row of symbols.
- Let them find those weather patterns which happened most and least frequently during the month.
- Review the Classroom Weather Calendar to see if there were any repeating weather patterns during the month.
- Show the videotape of last evening's TV weather report. See if the predictions made in this report actually come true.

Graphing the Weather *(cont.)*

Weather Graph

month_____   year_____

☀ **sunny**						
☁ **cloudy**						
⛅ **partly cloudy**						
🌧 **rain**						
❄ **snow**						

Building a Weather Vane

Overview: *Students will use a weather vane made by the teacher to determine wind direction.*

Materials

- 2 ½ inch (6.35 cm) Styrofoam ball
- meat skewers
- long, thin knitting needle
- plastic drinking straw
- coffee can with lid
- sand
- cardboard
- tape
- magnetic compass
- scissors
- Weather Vane Patterns (page 14)
- test tube or tall olive jar

Lesson Preparation

- Drive the knitting needle straight through the Styrofoam ball.
- Push the meat skewer into the ball so it is perpendicular to the knitting needle. The ends should stick out evenly on both sides of the ball.
- Trace the weather vane patterns onto cardboard and cut them out. Tape these to the ends of the meat skewer.
- Poke a hole in the center of the coffee can lid so it will hold the drinking straw in place.
- Place the test tube or olive jar in the coffee can and pour sand into the container to hold it upright and directly below the hole in the lid.
- Push the straw through the hole in the lid until it is inserted into the test tube or jar. Place the knitting needle through the straw and into the jar.
- Test to see if the weather vane has free movement by blowing on it. It should move even in a gentle breeze.

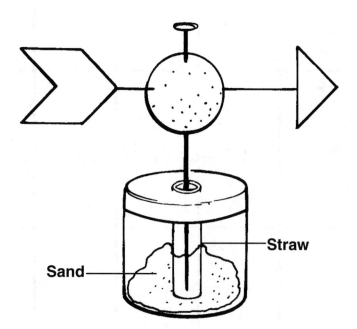

Sand ——

—— Straw

Building a Weather Vane *(cont.)*

Activity

1. Have the students look outside and tell you if the wind is moving. Ask them how they know (*trees or flag moving*).

2. Show the students the weather vane and take them outside to show them how it works. Do this on the playground or other area where buildings will not stop the wind.

3. Use the compass to find north. If available, find an area of pavement or dirt and draw the direction of north as an arrow. Place a line perpendicular to this line to show east and west. Mark this diagram with the letters **N, E, W, S**. The diagram is now a *compass rose*.

4. Set the weather vane on the diagram where the lines intersect. Have the students stand away from it and see which way it points. Explain that this is the direction from which the wind is blowing. Let them find the direction of the wind for that time.

Closure

- Return to the classroom and put the wind direction on the weather calendar, along with the other weather information.

- Have the students return to the area of the compass rose daily to find the wind direction and add this data to the weather calendar.

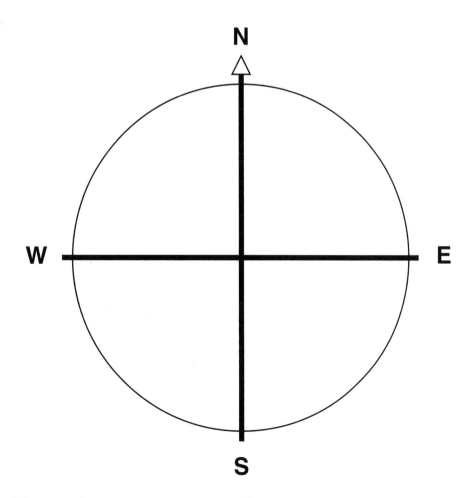

Weather Vane Patterns

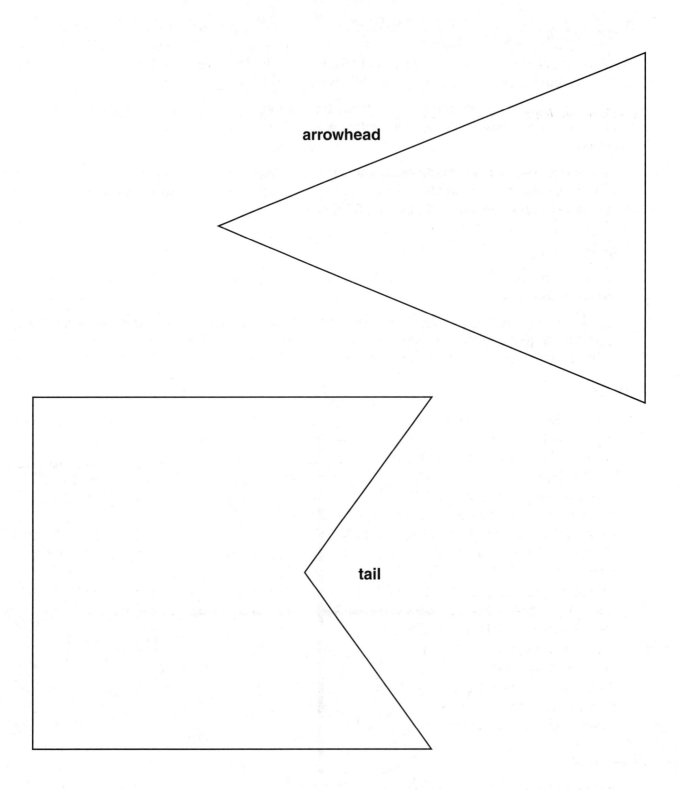

arrowhead

tail

Let's Go Fly a Kite

Teacher Information

Using lightweight, easy-to-fly kites is one of the best ways to let children experiment with wind currents. Although many patterns are available for homemade kites, inexpensive plastic kites work best for this activity.

Overview: *Students will use kites to study the wind.*

Materials

- inexpensive plastic kites (one for each pair of students and two extra kites)
- six-inch (15 cm) lengths of one-inch (2.5 cm) plastic irrigation pipe (one per kite)
- thick cotton string (available on a cardboard cone)
- classroom weather vane
- copies of Observation Record (page 16) for each student

Lesson Preparation

- Cut 50 feet (15 m) of string for each of the kites. Tie one end to the center of the kite according to the instructions on the kite, and the other to the center of the plastic pipe. Attach one kite to a string 200 feet (60 m) long. (*If possible, older students can assist in this activity.*)

Activity

1. Take students to a large field. Have them check the wind direction with the weather vane. Look at trees to see how the wind is moving the leaves and branches. Toss a handful of grass into the air so students can see the direction it blows.
2. Use the kite with the longest string to demonstrate how to fly a kite. Just as the children will do, have another person hold the kite up and release it when you are ready to run. When the kite is airborne, have students observe it move in the wind.
3. Explain that it is now their turn to fly their kites. Divide students into pairs in a line at one end of the field. The partners should stand face-to-face. The child who is to fly the kite will hold the pipe in one hand. The partner will hold the kite high by the center stick.
4. At a signal, the child holding the kite releases it, and the other partner runs down the field, gradually letting out string so the kite will climb. The other partner should run behind. Both should watch what the kite is doing as the wind catches it.
5. Have students practice in one part of the field to gain experience. It is best to let only a few practice at one time.
6. After students reach the far end of the field, they should line up again. This time, the other partner will get to fly the kite.
7. Provide time for students to observe their kites.

Closure

- Return to the classroom and have students use page 16 to make a series of drawings showing how they flew their kites. Have them write what they did to get the kite into the air and what helped to keep it up.

Let's Go Fly a Kite *(cont.)*

Observation Record

Name:_____ Date: _____

Draw three pictures which show how you flew your kite. After each drawing, write what you observed as you flew the kite.

1. This is how I began flying my kite.

_____

_____

_____

_____

_____

2. My kite is beginning to fly.

_____

_____

_____

_____

_____

3. My kite is successfully flying now.

_____

_____

_____

_____

_____

What Is a Cloud?

Overview: *Students will learn about clouds through a series of activities.*

Materials

- hot plate
- two pie pans
- ring stand or other device to hold one pie pan over the other
- water
- ice
- glass of water

pie pan with ice

pie pan with water

ring stand

hot plate

Lesson Preparation

- Place the hot plate on the table and put one pie pan on top of it. (An electric skillet can be used in place of the hot plate and one pie pan.) Pour in about one inch (2.5 cm) of water. Suspend the second pie pan above the pie pan with water in it. Put ice in this pan.
- This lesson will be done as a demonstration by the teacher. Arrange the students in the best position for them to observe the demonstration.

Activity (Do this activity on a sunny day.)

1. Ask students to tell you what they think of clouds are made and from where they come. Tell them they will begin a study of clouds today.

2. Take students outside to an area where there is pavement, preferably blacktop. Show them the glass of water and explain that you are going to spill the water onto the pavement. Have them predict what they think will happen. Pour the water and have them observe it. They should see that some of the water sinks into the pavement but most will spread out, leaving a wet spot.

3. Ask them to predict what they think will happen to the water as it is left to sit in the sunlight. Outline the puddle with chalk and tell the students that they will return to the classroom but will come back to this spot in a while to see what has happened to the water.

4. Return to the classroom and tell students that you are going to demonstrate how clouds form and what they are made from.

5. Point out the hot plate, the pan of water on it, and the pan of ice above it. Show that as the water heats, it turns into steam which rises. When the steam hits the cooler surface of the pan of ice above it, it begins to cool and turns into water droplets under the pan. Eventually, the water will begin to fall back into the pan on the hot plate.

6. Return to the area where the water was spilled on the pavement. Let students discover that the water has completely disappeared. Ask them where they think the water has gone.

Closure

- Have the students return to the classroom. Let them look at the hot water and ice demonstration again. Explain that the hot plate is like the sun which is heating the water. As the water heats, it begins to turn into steam, which is really droplets of water spread out into vapor. When it hits the pie pan above it, the vapor begins to cool off. Tell them the cold pie pan is like the upper atmosphere high above Earth. As the water vapor rises in the sky, it begins to cool and collects into clouds. If enough water vapor collects, it may begin to rain or snow, depending upon the temperature.

- Ask the children if any of them have ever flown in an airplane and flown through or near clouds. Explain that although the clouds look like cotton from the ground or from an airplane, they are really only water droplets which are very cold and thus usually in the form of ice crystals.

Where Is the Water Vapor?

Overview: *Students will learn that the air holds invisible water vapor.*

Materials

- ice
- food coloring
- clear container of water, at least one quart (1 L)
- thermometer
- white tissue handkerchief

Lesson Preparation

This lesson will be done as a teacher demonstration. Gather the students where they will able to observe the demonstration.

Activity

1. Ask the students what they learned about clouds in the previous lesson, What Is a Cloud?

2. Remind them that they saw water vapor being created by using the hot plate and the sun. Explain that today they will be able to see the invisible water vapor that is carried in the air around them.

3. Pour the water into the clear container. Add several drops of food coloring and stir until the color is mixed with the water. Show the students that the outside of the container is dry by running the tissue over it.

4. Take the temperature in the water and begin to add ice. Stir the water periodically. Add ice until water droplets begin to condense on the outside of the jar. Record the temperature on the board.

5. Wipe some of the water off with the tissue. Show the students that it is not the color of the water. Ask them where they think the water has come from. Did it leak out of the jar? (*No, or it would be colored water.*)

colored water with ice in it

Closure

- Remind the students that the water temperature dropped when ice was added to it. Explain that when the air hit the cold jar, the water in it began to pull together in the form of water droplets on the outside of the jar. Tell them this process is called *condensation*.

Dew Point

Teacher Information

The dew point is the temperature at which water vapor in the air will become cold enough to turn from a gas to a liquid.

Overview: *Students will learn about water vapor and the dew point.*

Materials

- empty coffee can
- water
- thermometer
- ice
- mirrors

Activity (This will be a demonstration lesson.)

1. Review what students learned in the lesson of "Where Is the Water Vapor?" Tell the students that they are going to find the temperature at which water vapor forms.

2. Tell the students who are wearing glasses to remove them, and distribute mirrors to the other students. Explain that you want the students to try an experiment. Have them open their mouths wide and then blow on the glasses or mirrors. Ask them what they saw on the glass (mist). Ask where the mist came from (the moisture in their breath).

3. Fill the coffee can with water and place the thermometer into the can. Read the thermometer and write the temperature on the board. Label it "water temperature—no ice."

4. Begin to add ice slowly to the coffee can. Watch the outside of the can for signs of "sweating", which is condensation. Immediately record the temperature on the board when you see the condensation. Label this "dew point temperature."

Closure

- Explain that when the water vapor formed on the outside of the can, the temperature of the water and the can had dropped and water vapor formed, just as it had in the jar in the previous lesson. Tell them that the temperature needed to form water vapor is not always the same. It depends upon the air temperature. If the air is colder and it meets a surface that is warmer, condensation can form. This sometimes happens if you are wearing glasses and walk from a warm house into cold air outside. The water in the air will condense on the glasses and they will "steam up."

- Have the students repeat the experiment with the mirrors and glasses. Explain that when the warm breath hit the cold surface of the mirror or glasses, it condensed the water from the breath into mist. When the mist formed, the dew point had been reached. Tell them to repeat this again and this time after the mist forms, watch it and count slowly to see how long it lasts. Have those who wear glasses put them on when the mist forms and count. (The mist on the glasses will evaporate faster since the body temperature is higher than the room.)

Sling Psychrometer

Teacher Information

The *relative humidity* is the amount of water that is actually present in the air and is reported as a percentage of the amount of water that could be in the air. You can find the relative humidity using a device known as a *sling psychrometer*. It is composed of two thermometers, one of which has a cloth sock on the bulb end and is wet before using the instrument. The dampness causes this wet thermometer to read a cooler than actual temperature. The difference in temperature between the dry and *wet thermometers* can then be interpreted, using a table, to determine the percentage of relative humidity.

Overview: *Students will construct a simple psychrometer.*

Materials

- drill
- four U-shaped clamps
- thermometer
- screws
- short stick
- small block of wood
- old shoelace
- thick string
- cup of water
- two small identical alcohol thermometers
- copy of Using a Sling Psychrometer (page 21)
- Percent of Relative Humidity Table (page 22)

Lesson Preparation

1. Drill a small hole near the top center of the block of the wood and at the end of the short stick. This is where the string will be threaded. (See illustration.)
2. Use the U-shaped clamps and screws to secure the thermometers to the small block of wood. Placed the thermometers parallel to each other and their bulbs pointed away from the hole. Be sure the bulbs project off the end of the block of wood.

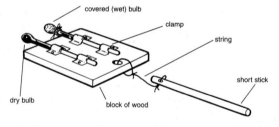

3. Cover the bulb end of one of the thermometers with a small length of the shoelace and tie it in place with a string. This will be the *wet bulb thermometer*.
4. Cut an 8-inch (20 cm) length of string and tie one end through the hole in the stick and the other end through the block of wood.

Activity

Take the students outside to earn how to use the sling psychrometer. Follow the instructions on using the sling psychrometer.

Closure

- Have the students record the relative humidity three times daily for a week. Ask students to check a TV weather report each day, before and after school, and then, record the relative humidity. Have them compare their results with those reported on TV.

Sling Psychrometer (cont.)

Using a Sling Psychrometer

Instructions: Use the sling psychrometer to determine the relative humidity in the air.

- Go outside and stand away from any objects (e.g., trees or people)
- Record the time of your test.
- Dip the bulb of the wet thermometer (the one with the shoelace tied to it) into water.
- Hold the psychrometer by the stick above your head and lightly swirl it in the air to the slow count of 20.
- Record the temperatures of both dry and wet bulb thermometers on the chart below. Calculate the difference between the two and record it. Refer to the Percent of Relative Humidity Table and find the relative humidity. Record this as a percentage (e.g. 59%).
- Repeat this five more times, with about one hour between each test.
- Compare what the relative humidity was throughout the day.

Sling Psychrometer Results				
Date/Time	Dry Bulb	Wet Bulb	Difference	*Relative Humidity
	°F	°F		%
	°F	°F		%
	°F	°F		%
	°F	°F		%
	°F	°F		%

Use the Percent of Relative Humidity Table on page 22 to find this information.

Sling Psychrometer (cont.)

Percent of Relative Humidity Table

Instructions: Use the sling psychrometer results to find the relative humidity from this table.

1. Find the dry bulb temperature on the left side of the table.
2. Find the difference between the dry and wet bulbs along the top of the table.
3. Move your fingers across the row and down the column until your fingers meet. Here, you will find the percent of relative humidity.

Example: Dry Bulb = 76 degrees/Difference between dry and wet bulb = 6/Relative Humidity = 73%

Percent of Relative Humidity (°F)
Degree Difference Between the Dry and Wet Bulbs

Temperature of Dry Bulb	1	2	3	4	5	6	7	8	9	10	11	12	13	14	15	16	17	18	19
98	96	93	89	86	82	79	96	72	69	66	63	60	57	54	52	49	46	44	41
96	96	93	89	85	82	78	75	72	68	65	62	59	57	54	51	48	45	43	40
94	96	93	89	85	81	78	75	71	68	65	62	59	56	53	50	47	44	42	39
92	96	92	88	85	81	78	74	71	67	64	61	58	55	52	49	46	43	40	38
90	96	92	88	84	81	77	74	70	67	63	60	57	54	51	48	45	42	39	36
88	96	92	88	84	80	77	73	69	66	63	59	56	53	50	47	44	41	38	35
86	96	92	88	84	80	76	72	69	65	62	58	55	52	49	45	42	39	36	33
84	96	92	87	83	79	76	72	68	64	61	57	54	51	47	44	41	38	35	32
82	96	91	87	83	79	75	71	67	64	60	56	53	49	46	43	40	36	33	30
80	96	91	83	87	79	74	70	66	63	59	55	52	48	45	41	38	35	31	28
78	95	91	86	82	78	74	70	66	62	58	54	50	47	43	40	36	33	30	26
76	95	91	86	82	78	73	69	65	61	57	53	49	45	42	38	34	31	28	24
74	95	90	86	81	77	72	68	64	60	56	52	48	44	40	36	33	29	26	22
72	95	90	85	80	76	71	67	63	58	54	50	46	42	38	34	31	27	23	20
70	95	90	85	80	75	71	66	62	57	53	49	44	40	36	32	28	24	21	17
68	95	90	84	79	75	70	65	60	56	51	47	43	38	34	30	26	22	18	15
66	95	89	84	78	74	69	64	59	54	50	45	41	36	32	28	23	20	16	12
64	94	88	83	77	73	68	63	58	53	48	43	39	34	30	25	21	17	13	9
62	94	88	83	77	72	67	61	56	51	46	41	37	32	27	23	18	14	10	5
60	94	88	82	77	71	65	60	55	50	44	39	34	29	25	20	15	11	6	2

Where Does Water Vapor Come From?

Overview: *Students will see that plants give off water vapor.*

Materials

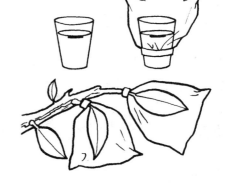

- three quart (liter) sized sealable plastic bags
- tree with large leaves on it
- two clear plastic 9-ounce (270 mL) cups
- copies of Water Vapor Data Sheet for each student (page 24)
- tape
- black felt marker

Activity

1. Review what students learned about condensation of water from the atmosphere in the lessons What Is a Cloud? and Where Is the Water Vapor?
2. Ask them how they think water vapor gets into the air.
3. Explain that water vapor can come from water evaporating from any moisture which is in the open air. Tell them they are going to do two experiments to see how water gets into the air.
4. Pour the same amount of water into the two clear plastic cups. Mark the level of the water in the cups with the black felt marker. Put a plastic bag over one of the cups and tape it in place. Tell the students that this experiment will take several days and that they will record what they see happening during that time.
5. Take the students outside to the tree. Let them watch you place the bags over two different leaves, sealing them around the stem of each leaf. Have them observe that there is nothing else inside the bag. Tell them that they will observe these leaves for a few days and record what happens to them.
6. Distribute two copies of the water vapor record sheet to each student. Let them begin by writing "leaves" on one form and "cups" on the other. Next, they should put the date, time, and their comments and drawings on the chart. If changes in either experiment occur before the school day ends, let the students update their records. If the students are too young to record their own data, make a class record on an enlarged version of the chart.

Closure

After students have observed and recorded changes in the water cups and bags on the leaves for several days, discuss what they have discovered. Explain what is happening.

- *The water in the open cup will drop below the black mark. This is due to the water changing to water vapor and mixing with the atmosphere—the process of evaporation.*
- *The water level in the cup covered by the plastic bag will not have dropped, but condensation will form inside the bag. This indicates that the water is evaporating but is unable to escape through the plastic bag.*
- *Water will begin to collect inside the bags which encase the leaves. Plants give off moisture through leaves, just as an animal does through skin. Normally this moisture is not visible since it evaporates as it oozes out. The plastic bag prevents evaporation.*

Where Does Water Come From? *(cont.)*

Water Vapor Data Sheet

Name:_____ Date: _____

These are my observations of the two_____.

Date	Time	Comments	Picture

What Are Those Clouds?

Overview: *Students will observe and identify clouds and record them on their weather calendar.*

Materials

- transparencies of Types of Clouds and Clouds in the Atmosphere (pages 26 and 27)
- sheets of cotton (available in drug stores) *optional:* large cotton balls
- white glue
- waxed paper
- toothpicks
- blue construction paper, $8^1/_2$" x 11" (22 cm x 28 cm)
- large-tipped black felt pens

Lesson Preparation

Make copies of the altitudes shown on the right side of the Clouds in the Atmosphere chart.

Activity (If possible, do this lesson on a day when clouds are visible.)

1. Take the students outside to look at the clouds. Let them sit or lie down and watch what happens to the clouds. If the clouds are moving, point this out to the students. Help them to see familiar objects (e.g., animals) formed by the clouds.

2. Return to class and show the transparency of the four types of clouds. See if the students can find any that match what they saw outside.

3. Show the transparency of the Clouds in the Atmosphere and explain to students that some clouds are lower than others. Point out those clouds which form high in the sky and those which are at lower levels. Explain that they are going to make a model of this picture, using cotton to represent the clouds.

4. Divide students into small groups and give each member a piece of construction paper and handful of cotton. Give each group a piece of waxed paper and white glue. Have them squeeze some of the glue onto the waxed paper. Give each child a toothpick and explain that each should use it to spread glue on the paper and then place the cotton over it.

5. Distribute to each student a strip with the altitudes on it. Have them glue this to the right edge of their papers.

6. Have the students glue cotton to their papers to represent the various clouds, following the chart. The black pen should be used to darken the undersurface of the cumulonimbus cloud. These are storm clouds and frequently appear dark underneath.

7. Let students copy the names and altitudes of these clouds on their charts.

(*Note:* If the students are too young to make individual cloud charts, the teacher should make one large one for display in the classroom.)

Closure

- Post the students' cloud charts on the bulletin board.
- On the weather calendar, write the types of clouds which were seen on this day. Continue to write the types of clouds on the calendar in the coming days.

Types of Clouds

The following illustrations show the three basic types of clouds and the cumulonimbus clouds. Below the illustrations, descriptions are given, along with explanations of how the clouds were named.

Cirrus clouds are high, thin, white clouds that are made of tiny ice pieces. *Cirrus* is a Latin word meaning curl.

Stratus clouds are low, flat gray clouds which are layered. When stratus clouds lie close to the ground, they are called fog. *Stratus* is a Latin word which means layer.

Cumulus clouds are white, puffy clouds which form in warm air on sunny days. They can quickly develop into thunder clouds or cumulonimbus clouds. *Cumulus* is Latin for heap.

Cumulonimbus clouds or thunderheads are huge, puffy, dark clouds, which are a type of cumulus cloud. *Nimbus* is Latin for rain.

What Are Those Clouds (cont.)

Clouds in the Atmosphere

This table illustrates several types of clouds and the heights they can reach in the atmosphere.

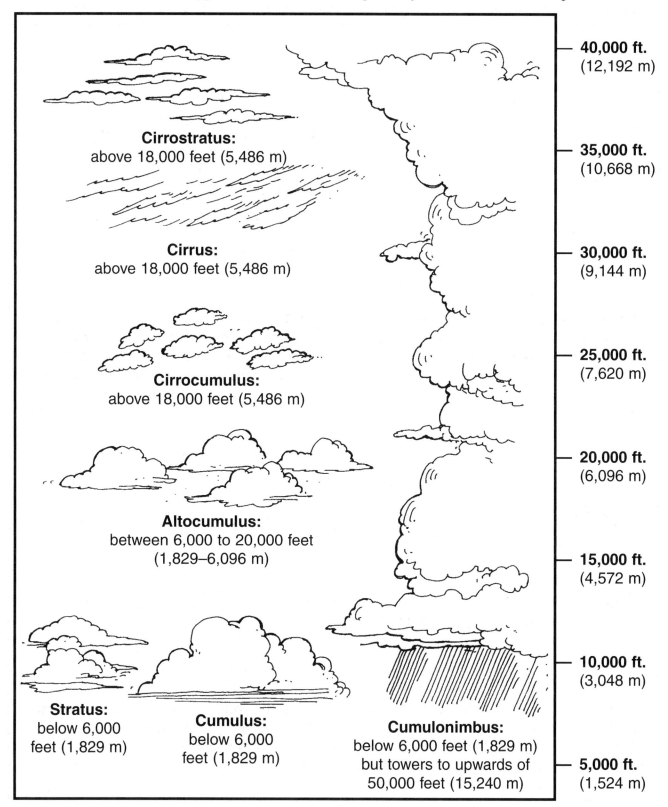

Cirrostratus:
above 18,000 feet (5,486 m)

Cirrus:
above 18,000 feet (5,486 m)

Cirrocumulus:
above 18,000 feet (5,486 m)

Altocumulus:
between 6,000 to 20,000 feet
(1,829–6,096 m)

Stratus:
below 6,000
feet (1,829 m)

Cumulus:
below 6,000
feet (1,829 m)

Cumulonimbus:
below 6,000 feet (1,829 m)
but towers to upwards of
50,000 feet (15,240 m)

— **40,000 ft.**
(12,192 m)

— **35,000 ft.**
(10,668 m)

— **30,000 ft.**
(9,144 m)

— **25,000 ft.**
(7,620 m)

— **20,000 ft.**
(6,096 m)

— **15,000 ft.**
(4,572 m)

— **10,000 ft.**
(3,048 m)

— **5,000 ft.**
(1,524 m)

How Are Clouds Formed?

Teacher Information

The information provided below should be shared with the students as they view the transparency of Cloud Formation. It will provide background for lessons that follow.

Overview: *Students will learn how clouds are formed.*

Materials

• transparency of Cloud Formation (page 29)

Cloud Formation Summary

Warm, moist air rises into the upper atmosphere.

1. The warm, moist air rises into the upper atmosphere.

2. Under the conditions of lower air pressure near the ground, the warm air expands, cools, and forms clouds.

3. All clouds form under these three conditions. But warm, moist air begins the process of cloud formation in one of the following ways:

Convection—When the sun warms the ground, the air above the ground is heated and begins to rise. This warm air, containing water vapor, rises in a process known as convection.

Since the upper atmosphere has less pressure than the atmosphere below it, the rising air and water vapor will expand and become cooler. The cooling water vapor forms a fog. Fogs that are high above the ground are called clouds.

Lifting—Clouds are formed by lifting when warm, moist air moves up the side of a mountain. Along its journey, the air is lifted higher into the atmosphere where the pressure is lower. Again, the water vapor in the air is allowed to cool and form a fog. This is why we often see clouds over mountains.

Frontal Activity—Sometimes a mass of warm, moist air, known as a warm front, will run into a mass of colder air, known as a cold front. When the two meet, the warm, moist air rises higher into the atmosphere. The lower pressure of the upper atmosphere causes the water vapor in the warm air to cool and form a cloud.

How Are Clouds Formed?

Cloud Formation

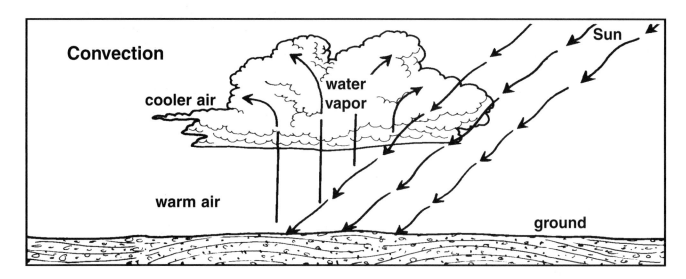

Convection

cooler air

water vapor

warm air

Sun

ground

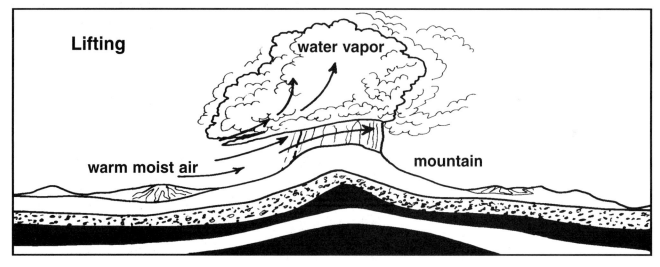

Lifting

water vapor

warm moist air

mountain

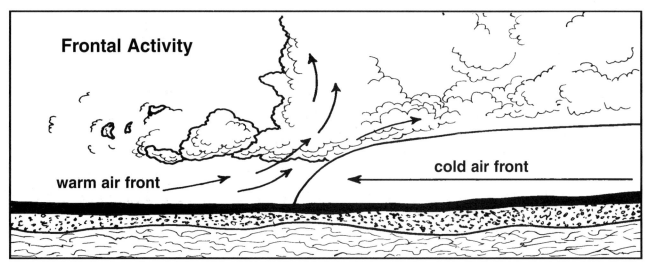

Frontal Activity

warm air front

cold air front

What Are Weather Fronts?

Teacher Information

Storms are caused when large air masses of different temperatures and moisture levels collide. The point where these two air masses meet is called a *front*. If cold air advances and pushes away the warm air, it forms a cold front. When warm air advances, it rides up over the denser, cold air mass to form a warm front.

The following demonstration illustrates what happens when a warm air mass collides with and replaces a cold air mass. The cooking oil represents a warm air mass and the colored water represents cold air mass.

Overview: *Students will learn about weather fronts.*

Materials

- clear glass cooking dish
- blue food dye
- cooking oil
- water
- scissors
- cardboard covered with clear plastic wrap
- transparency of Weather Fronts (page 31)

Activity

1. Cut the cardboard so that it forms a tight barrier between the right and left sides of the cooking dish. Wrap it with plastic wrap and seal the edges together as tight as possible. Place the barrier into the dish as shown in the drawing.

2. On the right side of the barrier, pour cooking oil into the dish so that it almost fills the right side.

3. On the left side of the barrier, pour water into the dish so that it almost fills the left side. Add a few drops of blue food dye to the water.

4. When the liquids appear calm, quickly lift the barrier and watch what happens.

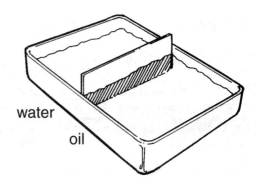

water

oil

Closure

- Have the students describe what they saw happen. (The cooking oil rose above the colored water when the barrier was lifted.) Explain that the cooking oil was like a warm air mass and the water was the cold air mass. Oil is less dense than water, just as warm air is less dense than cold air. Thus, when the two air masses of different temperatures met, the warmer one rose over the colder one.

- Tell the students that on Earth, warm and cold air masses are in constant motion due to the winds, particularly those winds in the upper atmosphere.

- Show the transparency Weather Fronts and discuss it with the students.

Weather Fronts

Cold Fronts:

Cold fronts form when dense masses of cold air advance into a mass of warm air and push the lighter warm air up out of its way. As the warm air rises, it often forms cumuli or cumulonimbi. These clouds are responsible for thunderstorms. This is why thunderstorms can often be seen along the leading edge of a cold front. Cold fronts typically move in a southeasterly direction across the United States.

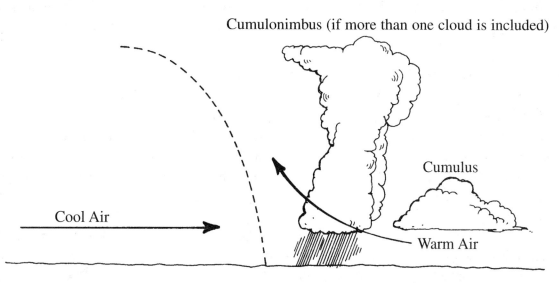

Cumulonimbus (if more than one cloud is included)

Cumulus

Cool Air

Warm Air

Warm Fronts:

When a warm air mass runs into a cold air mass, the warm air is forced to rise above the cold air. The transition zone where a warm air mass collides with and is replacing a dense cold air mass is called a *warm front*. This collision causes slowly rising clouds, such as cirri, altostrati, and strati. Generally, along the trailing edge of the warm front, nimbostrati are formed, which bring a drizzle or slow, steady rain to the area. Warm fronts typically move in a northeasterly direction across the United States.

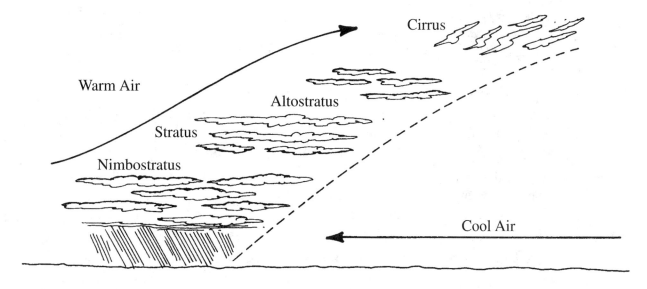

Cirrus

Warm Air

Altostratus

Stratus

Nimbostratus

Cool Air

Air Pressure

Overview: *Students will learn about air pressure.*

Materials

- transparencies of Clouds in the Atmosphere (page 27); Air Pressure and Elevation (page 33); Atmospheric Layers (page 35)
- full newspaper sheet
- two long, thin sticks (A paint stirrer works well.)
- table
- three 5-pound sacks of flour (represents 14.7 pounds)
- balloon
- colored paper cut into 1-inch squares

Activity

1. Review the transparency of Clouds in the Atmosphere.
2. Show and discuss the transparency of Air Pressure and Elevation.
   - Divide the students into small groups. Distribute 10 one-inch (2.5 cm) squares of paper to each group. Have them see how many of the squares will fit the arm and hand of someone in their group. Talk about how many squares would be needed to cover their entire body.
   - Let students hold the three bags of flour to see how heavy 15 pounds is. Explain that this represents the weight of the air pressing on every square inch of their body when they are at sea level.
   - Show the students the uninflated balloon. Ask them why it is flat. (It doesn't have anything inside it and is therefore pressed flat by air pressure.) Fill the balloon with water and tie it off. Have the students notice that the balloon stretches out in all directions with the water pressure inside it. Explain that their bodies are like that. The pressure inside their skin, mostly liquid, is pushing out against their skin in all directions at 14.7 pounds per square inch. Thus, they are not flattened by the air pressure pushing against them with 14.7 pounds of force from all directions.
3. Do the air pressure demonstration (page 34) to show the results of this pressure pushing against a newspaper. Ask the students to explain why the stick broke with just a light paper over it. (The air pressing down on every square inch of the paper was very heavy.)
   - After doing the demonstration, lay one inch squares on the newspaper to show their size compared to the newspaper. Measure the newspaper's length and width in inches and multiply these to find the number of square inches in the paper. Multiply the square inches by 14.7 to find the total air pressure on the paper.
4. Show and discuss the transparency of Atmospheric Layers.
   - Begin at the bottom of the chart at the troposphere layer and explain that this is the area shown on the Clouds in the Atmosphere transparency.
   - Read the information for each layer of the atmosphere and discuss it.
   - Point out that the Space Shuttle and International Space Station orbit about 150 miles above Earth. They are therefore well above the atmosphere.

Closure

- Have each student write a short illustrated story explaining what they have learned about air pressure.

Air Pressure (cont.)

Air Pressure and Elevation

Every square inch of your body is being pressed from all directions by 14.7 pounds of air pressure (at sea level) all the time. You do not feel it because you are used to it. As you climb a mountain or ride in an airplane, the pressure becomes less since you are moving higher into the atmosphere and less air is around you. Look at the picture below to see how the air pressure decreases as you climb higher into the atmosphere.

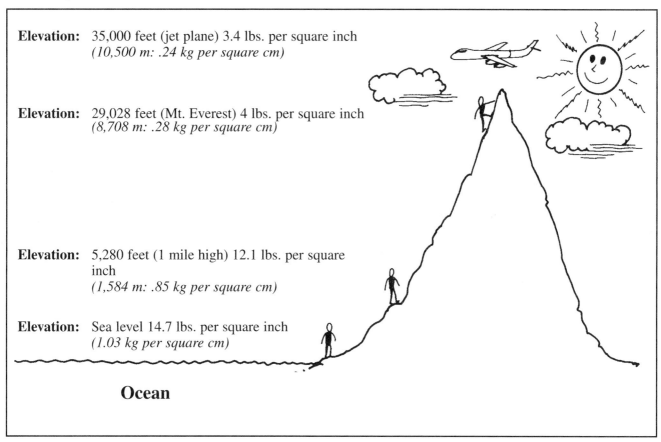

Elevation: 35,000 feet (jet plane) 3.4 lbs. per square inch
(10,500 m: .24 kg per square cm)

Elevation: 29,028 feet (Mt. Everest) 4 lbs. per square inch
(8,708 m: .28 kg per square cm)

Elevation: 5,280 feet (1 mile high) 12.1 lbs. per square inch
(1,584 m: .85 kg per square cm)

Elevation: Sea level 14.7 lbs. per square inch
(1.03 kg per square cm)

Ocean

Why do your ears sometimes pop when you go up or down in an airplane?

When you go higher into the atmosphere in an airplane, air pressure becomes less and less around you. Airplanes are pressurized to be like pressure on the ground and this changes gradually during take off and landing. When an airplane climbs or drops quickly, the pressurizing system takes a while to change the pressure in the cabin. The pressure inside your body always remains as it was on the ground so it is greater than that at higher elevations. This extra pressure fights to get out since it is now greater than the pressure pushing against you.

A tube leading from your inner ear to your throat, known as the Eustachian tube, allows air to pass into your throat to equalize the pressure when you swallow. When an airplane climbs or drops fast, the pressurizing system takes a while to return cabin pressure to normal. The pressure inside you is greater than the cabin pressure so it wants to escape. Air pressure begins to press against your eardrums and your ears feel as if they are plugged up. If you swallow, the air trapped behind your eardrums is equalized to the outside pressure and your ears "pop" and you can hear clearly again.

Air Pressure Demonstration

This demonstration will illustrate the amount of air that presses around us. The weight of the air is called air pressure and is measured in units of pounds per square inch. At sea level, there are approximately 14.7 pound of air on every square inch (1.03 kg per square centimeter) of ground or anything on the ground.

Materials

- full sheet of newspaper
- two long and thin sticks (paint stirrers)
- table

Procedure

1. Spread the full sheet of newspaper on the table.

2. Insert the stick under the sheet of newspaper so that half of the stick is projecting over the edge of the table, as shown in the illustration.

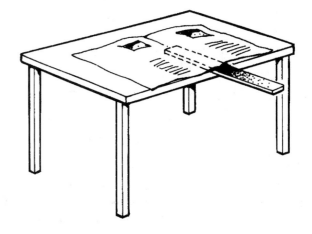

3. Using your fist, in a quick motion, strike down hard on the exposed end of the stick. If you struck quickly enough, the stick will break.

4. Repeat this with the second stick but hit the stick slowly. The stick will not break and the newspaper will fly up.

Closure

Ask the students to write an explanation for both observations (#3 and #4). Have them include labeled drawings with their explanation.

- The large surface of the newspaper will distribute the air pressure and make the paper incredibly heavy. An average sheet of newspaper has close to 10,000 pounds (4,500 kg) of air pressure on it!

- When the stick is struck rapidly, the pressure on the newspaper holds the hidden end firmly. A sudden, quick pressure on the exposed end of the stick breaks it.

- When the exposed end of the stick is struck slowly, air molecules roll off the newspaper, as if they were a bunch of marbles. This makes the pressure on the newspaper less. Striking it quickly does not give the air molecules a chance to get out of the way.

Air Pressure *(cont.)*

Atmospheric Layers

Thermosphere

Location: 50–70 miles (80.5–112.7 km) above the surface of the earth

Temperature Range: 2,192°F to 4°F (1,200°C to 20°C)

Facts: The thermosphere, also known as the ionosphere, is the highest layer of the atmosphere. Beyond the thermosphere lies the void of outer space. The aurora borealis, a spectacular electrical display, occurs in the thermosphere. Also, radio waves can be reflected by the thermosphere to carry signals farther.

Mesosphere

Location: 30–50 miles (48.3–80.5 km) above the surface of the earth

Temperature Range: –112°F to 68°F (–80°C to 20°C)

Facts: The mesosphere has the greatest range of temperatures in the entire atmosphere. It is generally warmer in its lower sections than in its upper sections. The aurora borealis also can occur in the upper mesosphere. High altitude helium weather balloons can reach into the mesosphere, but the air is too thin for airplanes to fly.

Ozone Layer

Location: 12–30 miles (19.32–48.3 km) above the surface of the earth (It is a part of the stratosphere.)

Temperature Range: 32°F to 68°F (0°C to 20°C)

Facts: Ozone is a poisonous gas for humans to breathe, but its presence in the stratosphere is important for all life on Earth. Ozone blocks harmful ultraviolet rays from the sun, which cause sunburns and can alter the DNA in plants and animals to cause genetic mutations. Recently, scientists have become concerned that chemicals known as chlorofluorocarbons (CFCs), found in aerosol sprays, refrigerators, and air conditioners, may be depleting the ozone layer. As a result, world governments have agreed to stop production of all CFC products by the year 2000.

Stratosphere

Location: 8–30 miles (12.8–48.3 km) above the surface of the earth (The ozone layer is located in the upper stratosphere.)

Temperature Range: –67°F to –40°F (–55°C to –40°C)

Facts: The powerful winds of the jet stream are located in the stratosphere. Major airline planes fly in the stratosphere. Since hardly any water exists in the stratosphere, there are no clouds at this level or any of the levels above it.

Troposphere

Location: 0–8 miles (0–12.88 km) above the surface of the earth

Temperature Range: –128°F to 136°F (–89°C to 58°C) near the earth's surface; –67°F to 68°F (–55°C to 20°C) in the upper troposphere

Facts: All of the earth's weather occurs in the troposphere. Non-jet airplanes fly in the troposphere. As a general rule, the temperature of the troposphere will decrease 3°F (5.5°C) for every 1,000 feet (300 m) of elevation.

Investigating Density of Air

Teacher Information

The density of air depends upon temperature. If air is warm, the air molecules move faster and spread out, making the air less dense or lighter and it will rise. Cold air is very dense since the molecules are more tightly packed, and will sink. Water molecules do this same thing, as this demonstration will illustrate.

Overview: *Students will learn about the density of air.*

Materials

- two clear glass bottles of equal size and shape (bottles used for iced tea work well)
- red food dye
- ice water
- hot water
- 3 x 5" (8 cm x 13 cm) index card

Procedure

1. Label one bottle "Hot" and the other bottle "Cold." Fill the bottle marked "hot" all the way to the brim with hot water. Add several drops of red food dye to the hot water and stir.

2. Completely fill the other bottle with ice water (but no ice cubes).

3. Place an index card over the top of the ice water bottle and hold it in place with your hand.

4. Quickly invert the ice water bottle over the hot water bottle and line up the necks of the bottles. (Do this over a sink or tray; it could be messy.)

5. The bottles should not be touching at their necks, but should have the card between them.

6. Have a student hold the bottles together as the card is carefully but quickly pulled out.

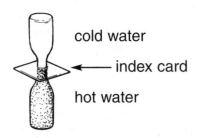

cold water

index card

hot water

Closure

After the students have watched the demonstration, let them explain what they think happened. (The hot water flowed up and the cold water flowed down. The hot water was less dense than the cold water.)

Prove to them that it was the water temperature that created the flow of water, not the dye.

- Ask what would happen if this were repeated with the hot water on the top. Conduct the experiment to show the results. (The hot water will remain on the top and the cold on the bottom.)

- Ask what would happen if the first experiment were repeated but no color was added to the cold water. Conduct the experiment to show the results. (The hot water would flow to the top and cold water to the bottom, exactly as it did in the first experiment.)

Investigating Density of Air *(cont.)*

Does Air Have Weight?

Teacher Information

This demonstration will show that air behaves just as the water did in the previous lesson. Thus, the students will develop a better understanding of how warm air rises and cold air sinks.

Overview: *Students will learn that air has weight that changes with temperature.*

Materials

- two paper bags exactly the same size (lunch bags work well)
- electric socket with 60-watt bulb (a "trouble" light may be used)
- simple balance beam
- two paper clips

Procedure

1. Place a paper clip on the bottom of each bag and bend it so that it becomes a hanger.
2. Hang each bag at the end of the balance beam, as shown in illustration A. Show that the beam hangs straight, demonstrating that the bags have equal weight.
3. Discuss what is filling the bags (air). Explain that the air inside the bags is the same temperature as all the rest of the air in the classroom.
4. Place the light under one of the bags and turn it on. (See illustration B.) Let the students watch what happens.

Closure

- Ask the student to make a drawing and label it to explain what happened here. (The bag over the hot lamp will begin to rise as the air gets warmer and expands, causing the bag to rise.)
- Discuss how this affects the air which makes up our atmosphere. (When the air get warmer, it will rise, as it get cold, it will drop.) This is what causes winds and clouds to move.

Balance Beam

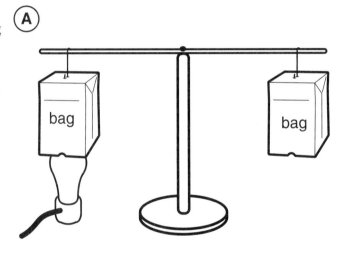

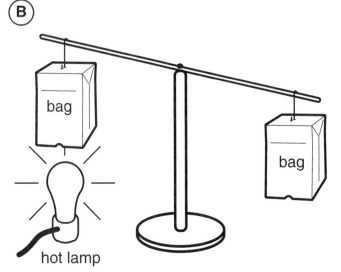

Investigating Density of Air *(cont.)*

Making a Parachute

Overview: *Students will learn more about the movement of air.*

Materials (per student)

- 12-inch (30 cm) square sheet of colored tissue
- clip on clothespin
- eight 12" (30 cm) pieces of light string
- (Optional: felt pens)
- 16 reinforcements for holes
- paper punch

Activity

1. Distribute the materials and explain that each student will create a parachute from these. Have them each fold the sheet of tissue into quarters. Punch a hole in the tissue at three locations as shown below. When the tissue is laid flat, eight holes should appear.

tissue folded into quarters

completed tissue paper laid flat

X

double folded side

Punch <u>half</u> holes at areas marked X.

● open edges

X

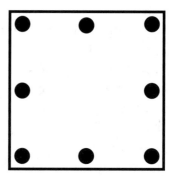

2. The students should put their names on their tissue and possibly decorate it with felt pens.
3. Have the students place a reinforcement circle on each side of the holes and then, attach one string to each hole. The strings should then be tied together at their ends and attached to the clothespin. The clothespin becomes the "person" who will ride on the parachute.

Closure

- Take the parachutes to the playground. Demonstrate one method for launching the parachute by holding the parachute in one hand and the clothespin in the other. Throw the pin and release the parachute at the same time. Have the students spread out. On a given signal let the students fling their parachute upward and watch them fall. Have them repeat this several times, watching to see where they go.
- Discuss what held the parachutes up (air) and where they went. The air may lift the parachutes briefly, if it is warm and rising fast.

Extender

- Experiment with different sizes of parachutes or those made from light fabric.

Hurricanes

Overview: *Students will learn how hurricanes develop, and are named and tracked.*

6. Pre-existing winds push the hurricane (in the Atlantic Ocean) northwest at speeds between 15–20 MPH (24–32 km/h).

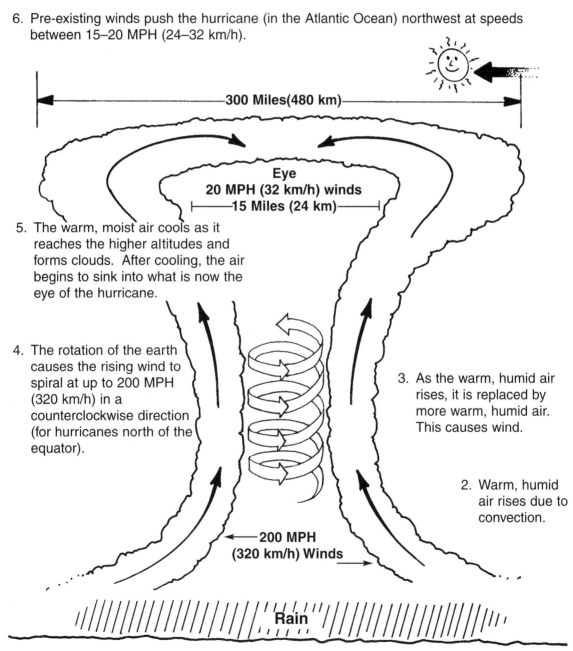

300 Miles(480 km)

Eye
20 MPH (32 km/h) winds
15 Miles (24 km)

5. The warm, moist air cools as it reaches the higher altitudes and forms clouds. After cooling, the air begins to sink into what is now the eye of the hurricane.

4. The rotation of the earth causes the rising wind to spiral at up to 200 MPH (320 km/h) in a counterclockwise direction (for hurricanes north of the equator).

3. As the warm, humid air rises, it is replaced by more warm, humid air. This causes wind.

2. Warm, humid air rises due to convection.

200 MPH (320 km/h) Winds

Rain

1. The ocean water must be at least 200 feet (61 m) deep and 80°F (27°C).

Hurricanes (cont.)

How Do Hurricanes Get Their Names?

Short, distinctive names for hurricanes in written and spoken communications are quicker and less likely to be mistaken, unlike the older more cumbersome latitude-longitude identification methods. Since 1953, Atlantic tropical storms have been named from lists made up by the National Hurricane Center. These are now maintained and updated by an international committee of the World Meteorological Organization. The naming of these storms began in the 1950s and featured only women's names until 1979, when men's and women's names were alternated. Six lists are used in rotation. Thus, the 2001 list will be used again in 2007.

The only time that there is a change in a name on the list is if a storm is so deadly or costly that the future use of its name on a different storm would be bring back bad memories. That storm's name is removed from the list and another name is selected to replace it. Some of the Atlantic storms which will never be used again and the year they occurred are: Andrew, 1992; Carmen, 1974; Gilbert, 1988; Hugo, 1989; Klaus, 1990: and Mitch, 1998.

North Atlantic Names

2001	2002	2003	2004	2005	2006
Allison	Arthur	Ana	Alex	Arlene	Alberto
Barry	Bertha	Bill	Bonnie	Bret	Beryl
Chantal	Cristobal	Claudette	Charley	Cindy	Chris
Dean	Dolly	Danny	Danielle	Dennis	Debby
Erin	Edouard	Erika	Earl	Emily	Ernesto
Felix	Fay	Fabian	Frances	Franklin	Florence
Gabrielle	Gustav	Grace	Gaston	Gert	Gordon
Humberto	Hanna	Henri	Hermine	Harvey	Helene
Iris	Isidore	Isabel	Ivan	Irene	Isaac
Jerry	Josephine	Juan	Jeanne	Jose	Joyce
Karen	Kyle	Kate	Karl	Katrina	Kirk
Lorenzo	Lili	Larry	Lisa	Lee	Leslie
Michelle	Marco	Mindy	Matthew	Maria	Michael
Noel	Nana	Nicholas	Nicole	Nate	Nadine
Olga	Omar	Odette	Otto	Ophelia	Oscar
Pablo	Paloma	Peter	Paula	Philippe	Patty
Rebekah	Rene	Rose	Richard	Rita	Rafael
Sebastien	Sally	Sam	Shary	Stan	Sandy
Tanya	Teddy	Teresa	Tomas	Tammy	Tony
Van	Vicky	Victor	Virginia	Vince	Valerie
Wendy	Wilfred	Wanda	Walter	Wilma	William

Closure

• Ask the students to see if they can find their names, or that of a friend in this list.

Winds and Hurricanes

Coriolis Effect

Teacher Information

The Coriolis Effect, is caused by Earth's rotation and determines the direction in which the atmosphere spins in the two hemispheres. Winds spin clockwise north of the equator and just the opposite south of it. However, hurricanes spin in a counterclockwise direction north of the equator and clockwise south of the equator. These storms are swept toward the west in the Northern Hemisphere and east in the Southern Hemisphere. (See diagrams below.)

Overview: *Students will learn how the spinning of the earth effects winds and hurricanes.*

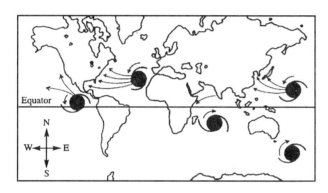

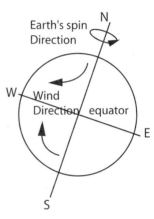

Materials

- globe
- white, self-adhesive dots
- washable red and blue felt pens

Procedure

1. Take the globe outside into the sunlight and have all the students stand around it. Explain that the sun appears to come up in the east and set in the west. This is caused by Earth turning west to east, or in a counterclockwise motion. Demonstrate this pointing out the spot where the sun is shining on the globe. Place three white dots in a line on the globe, one near the pole, one on the equator, and the other between the two. Spin the globe again and point out the dots so students can see the difference in their speed on the globe (Earth) at these three locations.

2. Explain that the Earth is about 24,000 miles in circumference (around the equator). It takes 24 hours for it to spin once in one day. A person standing at the equator would be spinning at a rate of about 1,000 miles per hour. However, someone standing at the poles would not be spinning at all. Spin the globe again and point out these areas so students can see the difference in speed of the Earth at these locations.

3. Show how this spinning effects the atmosphere by first drawing a line with the red pen from the North Pole to the equator. Now, spin the globe and, as it is spinning, use the blue pen to draw several lines in the same direction. Stop the globe and show the difference in the lines. The blue lines will curve toward the west. Repeat this but draw the lines from the South Pole to the equator. The lines will now curve toward the east.

Closure

- Discuss how the lines were pushed in the opposite directions in the hemispheres.

Tracking a Hurricane

Class Project

Overview: *Students will track a hurricane to simulate what meteorologists do.*

Materials

- seven copies and a transparency of page 43
- overhead projector
- small red self-adhesive dots
- transparency copy of hurricane shape on right
- copy of the pages 44 and 45

Lesson Preparation

Cut out the transparency of the hurricane shape. Mark a copy of the Hurricane Map with the locations of the complete data to create an answer sheet.

Activity

1. Tell the students that it is September 3 at 6:00 A.M. and information about a hurricane in the Atlantic Ocean near the Bahamas has just been received. The hurricane has been named Sam. Place the map transparency on the overhead. Find the coordinates for Hurricane Sam (20° N 64° W) and then, stick a dot on this location. Show the students how to find the coordinates as you do so. Put the transparency of the hurricane shape over the dot so that its center is over the dot. Let the students know that at this point, it has been decided that a hurricane warning and evacuation order will be sent to both the Bahamas and Dominican Republic. Show where these are located on the map.

2. Explain to the students that they are going to be meteorologists working at a hurricane center and following the progress of Hurricane Sam. Divide the students into six groups and provide each group a copy of the map, data pages, and six adhesive dots. Have them read the data and see that it is updated every 12 hours. Tell them to use the technique you showed them and plot the progress of the hurricane on their maps. Tell them to mark each new data on the map in pencil first and then, place the dot over it. Monitor the groups at first to be sure they understand what to do and are sharing the responsibilities.

3. Because students mark the new location each time, they should decide what action they will take such as, order evacuations or give only warnings. Discuss with them the consequences of giving evacuation orders as opposed to warnings.

Closure

- As the students work, plot the seven hurricane locations on the transparency, using the answer map prepared earlier. Discuss their answers for the warnings they gave as the hurricane progressed. These will vary with the groups. Lead the students in a final analysis of the hurricane warnings they gave. Help them understand how difficult this is in real life situations.

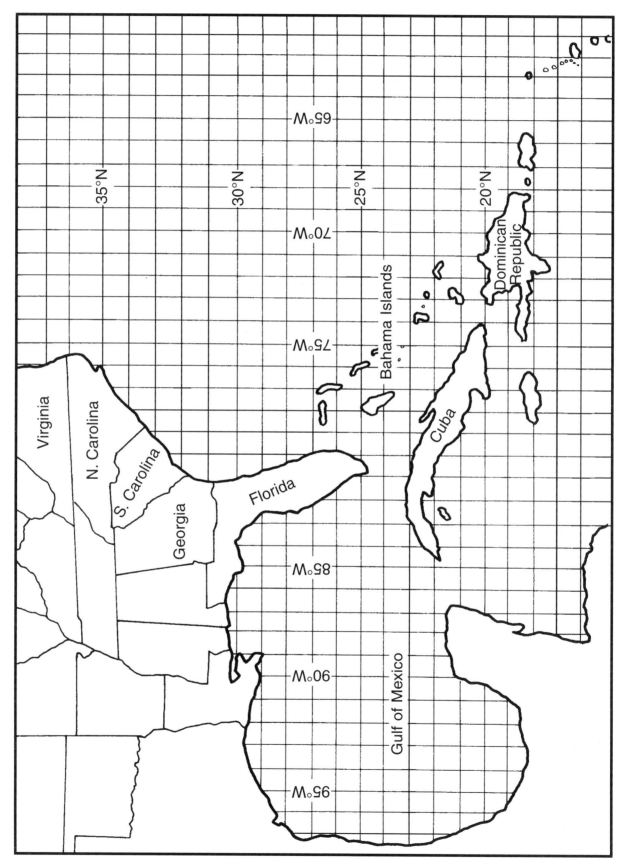

Map of Hurricane Site

Hurricane Sam Data

Time, Date, and Information	Location	Action
6:00 P.M. September 3 Hurricane Sam is picking up speed and power. It is headed straight for the Bahamas. The hurricane warning for the Bahamas was correct since it swept over the island.	22°N and 70°W	
6:00 A.M. September 4 Hurricane Sam is advancing rapidly northward. Speeds near the eye have been reported to be close to 150 mph (241 km/h).	24°N and 75°W	
6:00 P.M. September 4 The eye of the hurricane sits just off the coast of Florida. Mass destruction is occurring along the coastal areas. Forecasters are not sure of the direction the hurricane will take from here since hurricanes become unstable when they approach land.	27°N and 79°W	

Tracking a Hurricane *(cont.)*

Hurricane Sam Data *(cont.)*

Time, Date, and Information	Location	Action
6:00 A.M. September 5 Hurricane Sam has taken an abrupt turn northward and has avoided central Florida. It is still over the ocean and its eye is centered near the border between Florida and Georgia. Forecasters are fairly certain the hurricane will continue in its northerly path, as it is beginning to die down.	31° N and 81° W	
6:00 P.M. September 5 North Carolina is feeling Hurricane Sam. It looks as though the forecasters were right; the hurricane is continuing up the coast, but the land is slowing it down rapidly. Winds still beat against the coastline.	34° N and 77° W	
6:00 A.M. September 6 Hurricane Sam is dying down off the coast of Virginia this morning. Rains are striking the coastline, but the fierce winds which struck the Bahamas and Florida are now gone. Forecasters have downgraded the hurricane to a tropical depression. The worst is over!	37° N and 75° W	

Weather On the Internet

Overview: *Students will learn more about weather from Web sites.*

Materials

- access to the Internet
- colored printer

Lesson Preparation

- Visit the Web sites listed below before assigning these to students. Create specific items to look at, or activities to perform, when they visit the sites.

Activity

1. Divide the students into groups and provide each of them with one of the categories of Weather Internet Sites listed below. Provide sufficient time for them to visit these Web sites and gather information in the classroom and/or at home. Have them download and print copies of related graphics and pictures they can use in preparing presentations to the class.

Weather Internet Sites

Weather Reports

http://www.weather.com/

http://www.wunderground.com/

http://weather.yahoo.com/

http://www.usatoday.com/weather/wfront.htm

Names and history of hurricanes

http://www.fema.gov/kids/hunames.htm

http://www.nhc.noaa.gov/aboutnames.html

Coriolis Effect

http://www.discovery.com/area/skinnyon/skinnyon970523/skinny1.html

http://zebu.uoregon.edu/~js/glossary/coriolis_effect.html

http://www.usatoday.com/weather/wcorioli.htm

http://www.ems.psu.edu/~fraser/Bad/BadCoriolis.html

Atmospheric Pressure

http://www.usatoday.com/weather/wpress.htm

http://www.usatoday.com/weather/tg/whighlow/whighlow.htm

Closure

- Have the students present the information they learned about weather from the Internet sites they visited.

Extender

- Let them use this information in the Weather Report they prepare for the final lesson in this study.

Our Weather Report

Overview: *Students will create their own weather reports to give to the rest of the class.*

Materials

- weather calendars
- videotape of the most recent weather report
- props selected by the students
- homemade microphone or real one
- *optional:* video camera

Activity

1. Show the students the videotape of the weather report. As it goes along, discuss how the reporter is describing the weather and point out some of the things he or she uses to show the weather. Explain that the students will be writing their own weather reports, using some of the records they have made so far.

2. Discuss some of the ways students can report the weather, possibly even taking the class outside to look at the clouds. Help them think of a variety of ways to present the report and list these on the board.

3. Divide the students into small groups and have them brainstorm what information they will present and how they will report this to the class. Monitor the students' progress, offering suggestions and assistance as needed. Allow sufficient time for students to put their reports together, bring materials from home, and practice before presenting the reports to the class.

Closure

- Assign the groups to different mornings to give their weather reports. Invite the parents to visit during this time to see the results of the weather study.

Teacher and Student Resources

Suppliers of Science Materials

Delta Education   (800) 282-9560 Request a catalog of materials or order online at their Web site.
http://www.delta-education.com/corp/info/ordernow.html
Supplies a wide variety of materials to support hands-on science in all areas from elementary to middle school.

Great Explorations in Math and Science (GEMS)
http://www.lhs.berkeley.edu/GEMS/gemsguides.html
Directly from the Lawrence Hall of Science at UC Berkeley comes great teacher guides in a wide range of science topics. Check out their Web site to see all that is available.

National Science Resource Center   **http://www.si.edu/nsrc/**
Resources for Teaching Elementary Science. National Science Resource Center, National Academy Press, Washington, D.C., 1996. This outstanding resource guide to hands-on inquiry-centered elementary science curriculum materials and resources. Each reference in this guide has been carefully evaluated and is fully described, including addresses.
Read this book online or order it from: **http://www.nap.edu/catalog/4966.html**

National Science Teachers Association(NSTA) (800) 277-5300
http://www.nsta.org/ or the online catalog of materials at **http://store.nsta.org/**
This organization provides books, posters, and software related to astronomy and other sciences.
A monthly professional journal, the bimonthly NSTA Reports, discounts at the regional and national conventions, and an annual catalog of materials are available.

Resources

Nash, J. Madeleine. "Wait Till Next Time" *Time*, September 27, 1999. This article contains outstanding graphic which depict how a hurricane forms. It fully describes the possibility of more destructive storms in the Atlantic if global warming continues. This may be purchased from *Time* at their Web site **http://www.time.com/time/** In the search area at this site, type the title of the article to get information on ordering this article.